¡Mira cómo crece!

La vida de la manzana

Nancy Dickmann

Heinemann Library
Chicago, Illinois

www.heinemannraintree.com
Visit our website to find out
more information about
Heinemann-Raintree books.

To order:
☎ Phone 888-454-2279
▭ Visit www.heinemannraintree.com
to browse our catalog and order online.

Edited by Rebecca Rissman, Nancy Dickmann, and Catherine Veitch
Designed by Joanna Hinton-Malivoire
Picture research by Mica Brancic
Production by Victoria Fitzgerald
Originated by Capstone Global Library Ltd
Printed and bound in China by South China Printing
Company Ltd
Translation into Spanish by DoubleOPublishing Services

14 13 12 11 10
10 9 8 7 6 5 4 3 2 1

Library of Congress Cataloging-in-Publication Data
Dickmann, Nancy.
 [Apple's life. Spanish]
 La vida de la manzana / Nancy Dickmann.—1st ed.
   p. cm.—(¡Mira cómo crece!)
 Includes bibliographical references and index.
 ISBN 978-1-4329-5274-7 (hc)—ISBN 978-1-4329-5286-0 (pb) 1. Apples—
Juvenile literature. I. Title.
 SB363.D5418 2011
 634'.11—dc22   2010034141

Acknowledgments
We would would like to thank the following for permission to reproduce
photographs: Alamy pp. **9** (© Mode Images Limited), **10** (© Nigel Cattlin),
22 right (© Nigel Cattlin), **23 middle** (© Mode Images Limited), **23
bottom** (© Nigel Cattlin); FLPA p. **8** (© Nigel Cattlin); iStockphoto pp. **4**
(© Eric Michaud), **5** (© gaffera), **7** (© lillisphotography), **12** (© Ints
Tomsons), **15** (© Dmitry Ckalev), **17** (© Hayri Er), **19** (© Patty Colabuono),
20 (© Dianne Maire), **22 top** (© Dianne Maire), **22 bottom** (© Hayri
Er), **22 left** (© gaffera); Photolibrary pp. **13** (imagebroker.net/© Herbert
Kehrer), **14** (Garden Picture Library/© Mark Bolton), **18** (Animals
Animals/© Donald Specker), **21** (Garden Picture Library/© Mark Bolton);
Shutterstock pp. **6** (© Valery Potapova), **11** (© constant), **16** (© Gorilla),
23 top (© Gorilla).

Front cover photograph (main) of apples on a branch reproduced with
permission of iStockphoto (© Viorika Prikhodko). Front cover photograph
(inset) of a close-up of a green apple seed reproduced with permission of
iStockphoto (© Dianne Maire). Back cover photograph of apple flowers
reproduced with permission of iStockphoto (© Dmitry Ckalev).

The publisher would like to thank Nancy Harris for her assistance in the
preparation of this book.

Every effort has been made to contact copyright holders of material
reproduced in this book. Any omissions will be rectified in subsequent
printings if notice is given to the publisher.

Contenido

Ciclos de vida

Todos los seres vivos tienen un ciclo de vida.

La manzana tiene un ciclo de vida.

semilla

Dentro de una manzana hay semillas.
Las semillas se transformarán en un
nuevo manzano.

El nuevo manzano dará manzanas.
El ciclo de vida comienza de nuevo.

Semillas y brotes

La semilla de una manzana crece en la tierra.

raíces

Las raíces salen de la semilla y crecen hacia abajo, en la tierra.

brote

De la semilla nace un brote que crece hacia arriba.

hojas

Del brote salen hojas.

Convertirse en árbol

El arbolito necesita agua y luz solar
para crecer.

El arbolito se hace más grande.

Al árbol le salen hojas nuevas en la primavera.

flor

Al árbol le salen flores en la primavera.

Producir manzanas

polen

Llega una abeja a alimentarse en una flor. La abeja tiene polen sobre su cuerpo.

El polen ayuda a que nuevas semillas
de manzana crezcan en el árbol.

Luego comienza a crecer una manzana.

Cuando están maduras, algunas
manzanas caen del árbol.

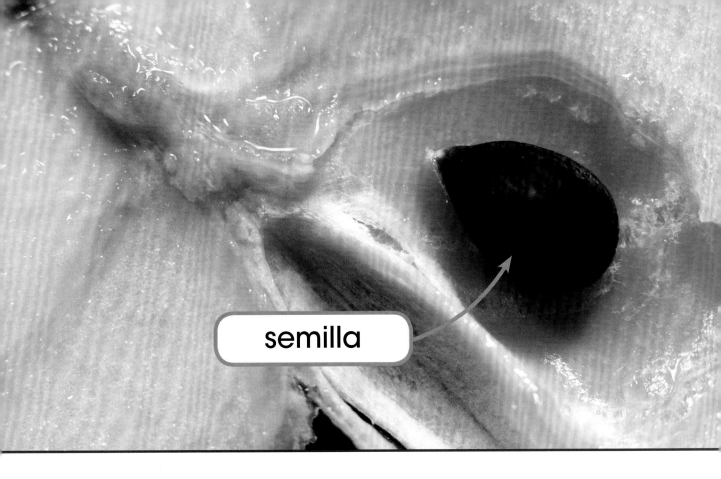

semilla

Dentro de la manzana hay semillas.

El ciclo de vida comienza de nuevo.

El ciclo de vida de un manzano

1 La semilla de una manzana crece en la tierra.

2 El arbolito se hace más grande.

4 Las flores se transforman en nuevas manzanas.

3 Al manzano le salen flores.

Glosario ilustrado

polen polvo amarillo que se encuentra dentro de una flor

raíz parte de la planta que crece bajo tierra. Las raíces absorben agua que usará la planta.

brote tallo pequeño y verde que sale de una semilla

Índice

Nota a padres y maestros

Antes de leer

Muestre una manzana a los niños y pregúnteles si saben cómo crecen las manzanas. Pregúnteles qué encontrarán adentro si corta la manzana en dos. Corte la manzana por la mitad y observen juntos las semillas. ¿Qué otra cosa conocen que crezca de una semilla?

Después de leer

• Hable con los niños sobre el Año Nuevo judío, Rosh Hashana. Explíqueles que es una tradición del pueblo judío comer manzanas bañadas en miel durante esta celebración, para tener un año nuevo dulce. Permita a los niños mojar un trozo de manzana en un poco de miel, así pueden probarlo.

• Cuente a los niños la historia de Johnny Appleseed y cómo plantó huertos de manzanas en Estados Unidos. Comente la importancia de plantar árboles nuevos. Quizás puedan plantar juntos un manzano en el patio de la escuela.

WHALES!

Written by Irene Trimble
Illustrated by Greg Harris

Reviewed by Lisa Mielke, Department of Education, New York Aquarium.

AN AMERICAN GREETINGS COMPANY

Manufactured for Learning Horizons, Inc.
One American Road, Cleveland, OH 44144. Printed in U.S.A.
Fabriqué pour Learning Horizons, Inc.
One American Road, Cleveland, OH 44144. Fabriqué Aux É.-U.
Cover design © 2001 Learning Horizons, Inc.

Visit us at: www.learninghorizons.com

SPLASH!

Imagine seeing an animal the size of a fire truck jumping out of the water and landing with a tremendous *SPLASH!* If you're lucky enough to go whale watching, that's just one of the amazing things you might see a whale do!

gray whale

There are 79 different species of whale in the world. The largest of them can weigh more than 30 elephants! Yet some of these awesome creatures will allow humans to touch them.

MAGNIFICENT MAMMALS

Whales are mammals, not fish. Like all warm-blooded creatures, whales have to breathe air to survive. They swim to the water's surface and breathe through a **blowhole**. A blowhole is like a nose on top of its head!

blue whale

Whales also have hair on their bodies and give birth to live young. Baby whales, called **calves**, drink rich milk from their mother's body. Some calves may gain as much as 200 pounds (91 kg) a day!

HOW THEY EAT

There are two kinds of whales: baleen whales and toothed whales. Baleen whales have a set of brushes in their mouths called **baleen plates**. They use the baleen to strain tiny plants and animals, called **plankton**, out of the water. Toothed whales have teeth to catch their food.

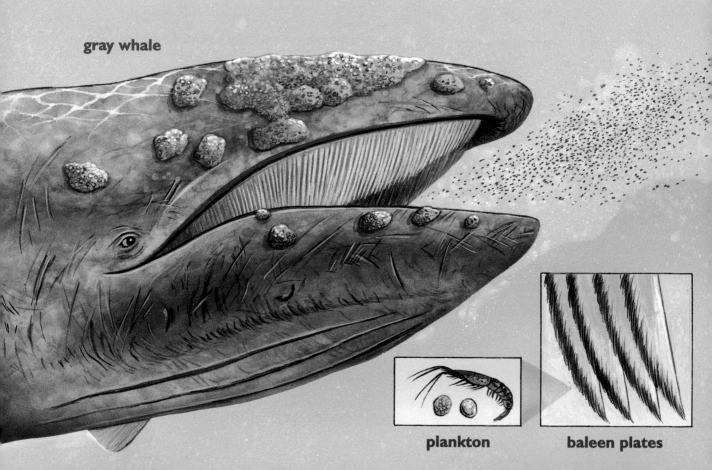

gray whale

plankton

baleen plates

Another way to tell whales apart is by looking at the tops of their heads! Baleen whales have two blow holes. Toothed whales have only one blow hole.

killer whale

GRAY WHALES

Gray Whales travel from the cold Bering Sea in Alaska to California, Baja, and Mexico to have their babies. This 13,000 mile (21,000 km) journey is the longest **migration** of any mammal. When a baby Gray Whale is born in these warm waters, it is 16 feet (5 m) long! That's a big baby!

 **Facts**

- Size: 46 feet (14 m) long, 35 tons (31.5 metric tons)
- Type: baleen
- Diet: crabs & other mud-dwelling creatures
- Found in the Northern Hemisphere

Gray Whales are the only baleen whales that feed from the bottom of the ocean. They suck in huge amounts of crabs, worms, and other animals that live in the mud.

BLUE WHALES

These enormous whales are the largest animals on Earth! Blue Whales can grow longer than two school buses put together. They can eat up to four tons (3.5 metric tons) of plankton and small shrimp, called **krill**, a day—that's like eating 32,000 hamburgers!

 **Facts**

- Size: 85 feet (26 m) long,
  100 tons (90 metric tons)
- Type: baleen
- Diet: plankton, krill
- Found in the Northern
  Hemisphere

Like most baleen whales, Blue Whales feed in cold
waters and then travel to warmer parts of the world to
breed and have their calves.

KILLER WHALES

Killer Whales are swift, deadly predators that live and hunt in family groups called **pods**. They swim at speeds of up to 34 miles per hour (55 kmh) and have 48 curved teeth for biting into their prey. They have even been known to come right out of the water to grab a seal on a beach!

Killer Whales are also called **orcas**. There is no record of an orca ever attacking a person in the wild—but they do eat other mammals!

 **Facts**

- Size: 32 feet (9.7 m) long, 8 tons (7.2 metric tons)
- Type: toothed
- Diet: fish, seals, sea turtles, dolphins, sharks, other whales
- Found worldwide

BELUGA WHALES

Beluga Whales live in cold waters where there is lots of ice, so their snowy white coloring makes them very hard to see. Believe it or not, they are sometimes attacked by polar bears!

 **Facts**

- Size: 16 feet (5 m) long, 1 ton (0.9 metric tons)
- Type: toothed
- Diet: fish
- Found in the Arctic

NARWHALS

Male Narwhals have a long spiral tusk that looks like a sword. This tusk is really a tooth that can grow up to 9 feet (3 m) long!

female narwhal

 **Facts**

- Size: 16 feet (5 m) long, 2 tons (1.8 metric tons)
- Type: toothed
- Diet: squid, fish, crab, shrimp
- Found in the Arctic

SPERM WHALES

You can tell Sperm Whales by their huge square heads, dark color, and wrinkled skin. They also have the largest brain in the world. An adult Sperm Whale's brain can weigh up to 20 pounds (9 kg)!

Sperm Whales sometimes battle and eat giant squid!
You can often see round marks left on their heads and
bodies by the struggling squid's tentacles.

 **Facts**

- Size: 59 feet (17.8 m) long,
  60 tons (54 metric tons)
- Type: toothed
- Diet: squid, fish
- Found worldwide

HUMPBACK WHALES

Can you tell a whale by its tail? You can if it's a Humpback! The two halves of a whale's tail are called **flukes**. No two Humpbacks have the same fluke markings, just as no two people have the same fingerprints. Humpback Whales have flukes that are 18 feet (6 m) wide!

Many whales make clicks, squeaks, and other vocalizations using their blow holes. Humpback Whales are called "singing whales" because their mating songs are so long and beautiful!

BOWHEAD WHALES

Bowhead Whales are the only large whales that spend their entire lives in the Arctic. Bowhead Whales can live in very cold waters because they have the thickest layer of fat of any whale! The fat, called **blubber**, keeps whales warm and cozy.

 **Facts**

- Size: 59 feet (17.8 m), 110 tons (99 metric tons)
- Type: baleen
- Diet: small fish, krill, plankton
- Found from the Arctic Ocean to the Bering Sea

Bowhead whales also have the longest baleen structure of any whale. With baleen plates that are 9 feet (3 m) long, they can scoop up a lot of krill and plankton!

BET YOU DIDN'T KNOW...

A newborn Blue Whale calf is 24 feet (7.2 m) long and weighs 2 tons (1.8 metric tons). It's the biggest baby in the world!

Sperm Whales spit up a substance called **ambergris**. It was once used to make perfume!

The Bowhead Whale has the biggest tongue—it can weigh over 1 ton (0.9 metric ton).

In the past, whalers called Gray Whales "devil fish" because the females used to destroy small boats that got between them and their calves.

Whales make sounds that help them locate food and find their way through the ocean. This is called **echolocation**.

Humans are still trying to unlock the many secrets of whales. We are just beginning to learn how deeply whales can dive, how far they can travel, and how intelligent these amazing creatures really are!